Azure DevOps 101

The Azure DevOps platform is a set of tools and services that help developers ship software faster and more reliably. It includes a hosted Git repository for source code, a continuous integration and delivery service, and a tool for managing application dependencies.

The book covers the following:

Chapter 1: Introduction to Azure DevOps

1.1 Understanding Azure DevOps and its Benefits

1.2 Overview of DevOps Principles and Practices

1.3 Key Components of Azure DevOps

1.4 Choosing the Right Azure DevOps Services for Your Needs

1.5 Setting Up an Azure DevOps Environment

Chapter 2: Azure Repos

2.1 Introduction to Azure Repos and Version Control Systems

2.2 Setting Up Git Repositories in Azure DevOps

2.3 Collaborating with Branching and Merging Strategies in Azure DevOps

2.4 Code Reviews and Pull Requests in Azure DevOps

2.5 Integrating External Git Repositories in Azure DevOps

Chapter 3: Azure Boards

3.1 Managing Work Items and Agile Planning in Azure DevOps

3.2 Creating and Tracking Backlogs and User Stories in Azure DevOps

3.3 Setting Up Kanban Boards and Task Boards in Azure DevOps

3.4 Agile Reporting and Metrics in Azure DevOps

3.5 Integrating Azure Boards with Development Processes in Azure DevOps

Chapter 4: Azure Pipelines (Part 1: Fundamentals)

4.1 Introduction to Azure Pipelines and Continuous Integration/Continuous Delivery (CI/CD)

4.2 Configuring Build Pipelines for Continuous Integration in Azure DevOps

4.3 Building and Packaging Applications in Azure DevOps

4.4 Running Automated Tests in Pipelines in Azure DevOps

4.5 Managing Pipeline Environments and Variables in Azure DevOps

Chapter 5: Azure Pipelines (Part 2: Advanced Topics)

5.1 Deploying Applications with Release Pipelines in Azure DevOps

5.2 Creating Environments and Managing Deployment Strategies in Azure DevOps

5.3 Automating Infrastructure Provisioning and Deployment in Azure DevOps

5.4 Implementing Approval Gates and Release Policies in Azure DevOps

5.5 Monitoring and Troubleshooting Pipelines in Azure DevOps

Chapter 6: Azure Test Plans

6.1 Overview of Azure Test Plans and Test Management in Azure DevOps

6.2 Creating Test Plans and Test Suites in Azure DevOps

6.3 Test Case Management and Execution in Azure DevOps

6.4 Exploratory Testing and Session-based Testing in Azure DevOps

6.5 Integrating Automated Testing in Test Plans in Azure DevOps

Chapter 7: Azure Artifacts

7.1 Introduction to Azure Artifacts and Package Management

7.2 Setting Up Package Feeds and NuGet Repositories in Azure DevOps

7.3 Publishing and Managing Packages in Azure DevOps

7.4 Package Versioning and Dependency Management in Azure DevOps

7.5 Integrating Artifacts with Build and Release Pipelines in Azure DevOps

Chapter 8: Azure DevOps Extensions and Integrations

8.1 Extending Azure DevOps with Marketplace Extensions

8.2 Exploring Commonly Used Extensions in Azure DevOps

8.3 Creating Custom Extensions for Azure DevOps

8.4 Integrating Azure DevOps with Third-Party Tools and Services

Chapter 9: Infrastructure as Code with Azure DevOps

9.1 Introduction to Infrastructure as Code (IaC) Concepts in Azure DevOps

Chapter 11: Azure DevOps for Multi-team and Enterprise Environments

11.1 Scaling Azure DevOps for Large Projects and Multiple Teams

11.2 Managing Permissions and Access Control in Azure DevOps

11.3 Configuring Branch Policies and Code Reviews for Collaboration in Azure DevOps

11.4 Setting Up Governance and Compliance Standards in Azure DevOps

11.5 Implementing DevOps Best Practices in Enterprise Environments in Azure DevOps

Chapter 12: Continuous Improvement and Future Trends in Azure DevOps

12.1 Embracing a Culture of Continuous Improvement in Azure DevOps

12.2 Monitoring and Analyzing DevOps Metrics and Performance in Azure DevOps

12.3 Identifying and Addressing Bottlenecks in the Azure DevOps Workflow

12.4 DevOps Trends and Innovations

12.5 Enhancing Collaboration and Integration with Azure DevOps

The Azure DevOps platform is a set of tools and services that help developers ship software faster and more reliably. It includes a hosted Git repository for source code, a continuous integration and delivery service, and a tool for managing application dependencies.

Azure DevOps is a cloud-based service that provides a set of tools to manage software development projects from start to finish. These tools include a hosted Git repository for source code, a continuous integration and delivery service, and a tool for managing application dependencies. Azure DevOps makes it easy to track work progress and collaborate with others on your team.

As your team begins to use Azure DevOps, you will want to familiarize yourself with the platform and how it can help you ship software faster and more reliably. In this chapter, we will cover the following topics:

- What is Azure DevOps?
- What are the benefits of using Azure DevOps?
- What tools and services are included in Azure DevOps?

- How can I get started with Azure DevOps?

1.1 Understanding Azure DevOps and its Benefits

There are many benefits to using Azure DevOps, including the ability to collaborate with others on code development, the ability to track and manage code changes, and the ability to deploy code changes easily and quickly. Azure DevOps also provides a number of other features and benefits that can be extremely helpful for developers, including the ability to automatically build and test code changes, the ability to manage code branches, and the ability to easily share code changes with others. Overall, Azure DevOps can be a great tool for developers of all experience levels who are looking to improve their code development process.

1.2 Overview of DevOps Principles and Practices

The following is an overview of DevOps principles and practices as related to the software development process.

DevOps is a set of practices that combines software development (Dev) and information technology operations (Ops) to shorten the software development life cycle and deliver features, fixes, and updates faster and more frequently.

The main goal of DevOps is to increase the speed and quality of software delivery while reducing the time it takes to go from idea to market.

DevOps is accomplished by automating and monitoring the entire software development process, from development and testing to deployment and operations.

DevOps enables organizations to rapidly and safely deliver software products and updates to customers.

The key benefits of DevOps include:

- Increased speed and quality of software delivery
- Reduced time to market
- Improved customer satisfaction
- Increased collaboration between development and operations teams
- Improved communication and transparency

The main principles of DevOps include:

- Automation
- Monitoring
- Continuous Delivery
- Continuous Integration
- DevOps culture

1.3 Key Components of Azure DevOps

Azure DevOps is a set of tools and services that help you develop and deploy software in the cloud. It includes a set of tools for managing code, building and testing software, and deploying and monitoring applications. Azure DevOps also provides a set of services for collaboration, such as

work item tracking, version control, and build
services.

1.4 Choosing the Right Azure DevOps Services for Your Needs

There are many different Azure DevOps services available, and it can be difficult to decide which ones are right for your needs. In this article, we'll take a look at some of the most popular Azure DevOps services and how they can help you streamline your development process.

Azure Pipelines is a popular choice for Continuous Integration and Continuous Delivery (CI/CD). It can be used to automate the build, test, and deploy process for your applications. Azure Pipelines is highly scalable and can be used to build and deploy applications to any platform, including on-premises and cloud-based environments.

Azure Boards is a great choice for project and product managers who need to track work items, Kanban boards, and sprints. Azure Boards also integrates with Azure Pipelines, so you can see the status of your builds and deployments in one place.

Azure Artifacts is a package management service that can be used to store and share packages across your organization. Azure Artifacts is compatible with popular package managers like NuGet and npm, and it integrates with Azure Pipelines, so you can automate the creation and deployment of packages.

Azure Test Plans is a great choice for teams who need to plan, execute, and track their testing efforts. Azure Test Plans integrates with Azure Pipelines, so you can run automated tests as part of your CI/CD pipeline.

If you're looking for a complete DevOps solution, Azure DevOps Services is a great choice. Azure DevOps Services includes all of the above services, plus many more, in one integrated platform. Azure DevOps Services makes it easy to get started with DevOps, and it's a great choice for teams of all sizes.

1.5 Setting Up an Azure DevOps Environment

As a new developer, I was excited to learn about Azure DevOps and how it could help me streamline my workflow. After some research, I decided to set up an Azure DevOps environment for myself.

First, I created a new Azure DevOps account and a new project. I gave my project a name and description, and then I set up my git repository. Next, I installed the Azure DevOps extension for Visual Studio Code.

With the extension installed, I was able to connect my local development environment to my Azure DevOps account. This allowed me to push my code changes to my Azure DevOps repository and track my work in the Azure DevOps interface.

Overall, I'm very happy with my new Azure DevOps environment. It's helped me to keep my code changes organized and has made collaborating with other developers much easier.

Chapter 2: Azure Repos

2.1 Introduction to Azure Repos and Version Control Systems

Version control systems are software tools that help a software team manage changes to source code over time. Azure Repos is a cloud-based version control system that allows you to collaborate on code with your team and take advantage of powerful Azure DevOps features. In this chapter, you will learn about the basics of using Azure Repos and how to use it to manage your code.

2.2 Setting Up Git Repositories in Azure DevOps

In Azure DevOps, a Git repository is a perfect way to manage your application's source code. By using a Git repository, you can easily track changes to your code, collaborate with others, and easily roll back changes if needed.

To set up a Git repository in Azure DevOps, you first need to create a new project. To do this, log into the Azure DevOps portal and click on the "New Project" button.

Give your project a name and description, then click on the "Create" button.

Once your project has been created, you'll be taken to the project's dashboard. From here, click on the "Repos" tab.

On the "Repos" page, you'll see a list of all the repositories in your project. To create a new repository, click on the "New Repository" button.

Give your repository a name, then click on the "Create" button.

Your new repository will now be created and you'll be taken to the repository's main page.

From here, you can start adding files to your repository. To do this, click on the "Add" button.

On the "Add to Repository" page, select the "Add an existing file" option.

Browse to the location of the file you want to add, select it, and then click on the "Add" button.

Your file will now be added to the repository and you'll be able to see it in the "Files" section.

You can now continue adding files to your repository or start working with them. To learn more about working with Git repositories in Azure DevOps, check out the documentation.

2.3 Collaborating with Branching and Merging Strategies in Azure DevOps

Branching and merging strategies are key to collaborating effectively in Azure DevOps. By understanding and utilizing these strategies, developers can work together more efficiently and avoid potential conflicts.

When working with branches, it is important to consider the purpose of the branch. For example, if a developer is working on a new feature, they would likely create a new branch for their work. This allows other developers to continue working on the main branch without having to worry about the new feature being developed. Once the new feature is completed, it can then be merged into the main branch.

There are several different ways to merge branches, and the best approach depends on the situation. In some cases, it may be best to simply merge the changes from one branch into another.

However, in other cases, it may be necessary to first rebase the changes onto the main branch before merging. This can help to avoid potential conflicts and ensure that all changes are included in the final merge.

No matter what approach is taken, it is important to always communicate with other developers when working with branches. This way, everyone is aware of what is happening and can avoid potential conflicts. By following these simple strategies, collaborating in Azure DevOps can be a much smoother process.

2.4 Code Reviews and Pull Requests in Azure DevOps

Code reviews and pull requests are an important part of the Azure DevOps process. They help ensure that code changes are reviewed and approved by other members of the team before they are merged into the main codebase. This helps to avoid potential problems that could occur if code changes were made without proper review.

Code reviews can be performed using the Azure DevOps web interface or through the use of the git command line tool. To perform a code review using the web interface, navigate to the Code tab of the Azure DevOps project and select the file or files that you would like to review. Click on the Review button and enter your comments. Once you are finished, click the Submit button to submit your review.

To perform a code review using the git command line tool, use the git review command. This will open up a web page where you can enter your comments. Once you are finished, click the Submit button to submit your review.

2.5 Integrating External Git Repositories in Azure DevOps

In Azure DevOps, you can easily integrate with external Git repositories. This allows you to keep your code in sync with code from other repositories.

To integrate with an external Git repository, you first need to add it as a remote. To do this, open the Azure DevOps portal and go to your project. Under the "Repos" section, click on the "Remotes" tab.

Click the "Add" button to add a new remote. In the "Name" field, enter the name of the remote. In the

"URL" field, enter the URL of the external Git repository.

Once the remote has been added, you can push and pull code to and from the external repository. To do this, go to the "Changes" tab in the Azure DevOps portal.

Make sure that the "Push" option is selected. Enter a commit message and click the "Commit" button.

Your code will now be pushed to the external Git repository.

Chapter 3: Azure Boards

3.1 Managing Work Items and Agile Planning in Azure DevOps

As a developer, one of the most important things you can do is manage your work items and agile planning in Azure DevOps. By doing so, you can ensure that your work is properly tracked and that you are able to stay on top of your agile planning.

To manage your work items and agile planning in Azure DevOps, you will first need to go to the Azure Boards section of the Azure DevOps portal. Once there, you will be able to see all of your work items as well as your agile planning.

To view your work items, simply click on the "Work Items" tab. Here, you will be able to see all of the work items that have been assigned to you as well as those that are currently in progress. You can also view work items that have been completed by clicking on the "Completed" tab.

To view your agile planning, click on the "Agile Planning" tab. Here, you will be able to see all of the agile planning that has been assigned to you.

You can also view agile planning that has been completed by clicking on the "Completed" tab.

By managing your work items and agile planning in Azure DevOps, you can ensure that your work is properly tracked and that you are able to stay on top of your agile planning. This will ultimately help you to be more productive and efficient in your work.

3.2 Creating and Tracking Backlogs and User Stories in Azure DevOps

As a product owner, I want to be able to create and track backlogs and user stories in Azure DevOps so that I can keep track of the development of my product.

Creating and tracking backlogs and user stories in Azure DevOps is a simple process. First, I create a new product backlog item and give it a name and description. Then, I add the user story to the backlog item. I can track the progress of the user story by looking at the work items associated with it.

As the product owner, I can also add tasks to the user story. I can assign these tasks to developers and track their progress. I can also add acceptance criteria to the user story. This helps me to ensure that the user story is developed according to my expectations.

Creating and tracking backlogs and user stories in Azure DevOps is a great way to keep track of the development of my product. It helps me to ensure that my product is being developed according to my expectations and that it is on track for delivery.

3.3 Setting Up Kanban Boards and Task Boards in Azure DevOps

As a team lead, you're responsible for setting up and configuring Azure DevOps for your team. In this section, you'll learn how to set up Kanban boards and task boards in Azure DevOps.

Kanban boards help you visualize your work, and task boards help you track and manage your work items.

To set up a Kanban board, go to your project in Azure DevOps and select Boards>Kanban Boards>New Kanban Board.

Give your Kanban board a name and description, and then select the work item types that you want to include on the board.

To set up a task board, go to your project in Azure DevOps and select Boards>Task Boards>New Task Board.

Give your task board a name and description, and then select the work item types that you want to include on the board.

Task boards can be used to track work items across multiple projects. To add a project to a task board, go to the board settings and select the projects that you want to add.

You can also add swimlanes to your task boards to help you organize your work. Swimlanes can be used to group work items by assignee, work item type, or any other field.

To add a swimlane, go to the board settings and select the swimlane type that you want to add.

Now that you've learned how to set up Kanban boards and task boards in Azure DevOps, you're ready to start tracking and managing your work items.

3.4 Agile Reporting and Metrics in Azure DevOps

The Azure Boards service enables agile teams to track their work and collaborate effectively. The service provides a rich set of features for planning, tracking, and managing work. Azure Boards also provides robust reporting and metrics capabilities that help teams track their progress and identify areas of improvement.

The reporting and metrics features in Azure Boards are designed to provide insights into the work of agile teams. The reports and metrics help teams track their progress, identify areas of improvement, and make informed decisions about their work. Azure Boards provides a variety of reports and metrics that can be customized to meet the needs of individual teams.

The Azure Boards service enables teams to track their work and collaborate effectively. The service provides a rich set of features for planning, tracking, and managing work. Azure Boards also provides robust reporting and metrics capabilities that help teams track their progress and identify areas of improvement.

The reporting and metrics features in Azure Boards are designed to provide insights into the work of agile teams. The reports and metrics help teams track their progress, identify areas of improvement, and make informed decisions about their work. Azure Boards provides a variety of reports and metrics that can be customized to meet the needs of individual teams.

The Azure Boards service enables teams to track their work and collaborate effectively. The service provides a rich set of features for planning, tracking, and managing work. Azure Boards also provides robust reporting and metrics capabilities that help teams track their progress and identify areas of improvement.

The reporting and metrics features in Azure Boards are designed to provide insights into the work of agile teams. The reports and metrics help teams track their progress, identify areas of improvement, and make informed decisions about their work. Azure Boards provides a variety of reports and metrics that can be customized to meet the needs of individual teams.

3.5 Integrating Azure Boards with Development Processes in Azure DevOps

As a development team starts to use Azure DevOps, they will quickly find that Azure Boards is a valuable tool for managing their work. By integrating Azure Boards with their development process, they can get even more out of the tool.

The first step is to create a board for each development process. For example, if the team has a process for feature development and another for bug fixes, they should create a board for each. This will help keep the work organized and make it easier to track progress.

Once the boards are set up, the team can start adding work items. For each work item, they can assign it to a specific developer and set a due date. They can also add comments and attachments to keep everyone on the same page.

As work items are completed, the team can move them to the appropriate column on the board. This will help everyone see the progress that is being made and identify any areas that need more attention.

By integrating Azure Boards with their development process, the team can get a better overview of their work and make sure that everything is on track. This will help them deliver high-quality software products to their customers.

Chapter 4: Azure Pipelines (Part 1: Fundamentals)

4.1 Introduction to Azure Pipelines and Continuous Integration/Continuous Delivery (CI/CD)

Continuous Integration (CI) is a development practice that requires developers to integrate code into a shared repository several times a day. Each check-in is then verified by an automated build, allowing teams to detect problems early.

Continuous Delivery (CD) takes CI one step further by automating the release process. This means that once code is merged into the shared repository, it is automatically deployed to a staging or production environment. CD helps reduce the risk of human error and ensures that software is always up-to-date.

Azure Pipelines is a cloud-based CI/CD service that automates the build, test, and release process. Azure Pipelines can be used with any language, platform, or cloud. In this chapter, we will cover the basics of Azure Pipelines and show you how to set up a simple CI/CD pipeline.

4.2 Configuring Build Pipelines for Continuous Integration in Azure DevOps

In Azure DevOps, you can create build pipelines for continuous integration (CI). CI pipelines automatically build and test your code every time you commit changes. This helps ensure that your code is always up to date and compliant with your organization's standards.

To create a CI pipeline, you first need to create a new Azure DevOps project. Then, go to the Pipelines tab and click on the New Pipeline button. In the next screen, you will need to select a source control provider. For this example, we will use GitHub.

Once you have selected your source control provider, you will need to select a repository. For this example, we will use the Azure DevOps Demo Repository.

After you have selected your repository, you will need to choose a template for your pipeline. For this example, we will use the ASP.NET Core template.

In the next screen, you will need to provide a name for your pipeline and select the branch that you want to build. For this example, we will use the master branch.

Once you have provided a name for your pipeline and selected the branch that you want to build, you will need to click on the Save & Queue button. This will save your pipeline and queue a build.

Once the build has been queued, you can monitor the progress of the build in the Builds tab. Once the build has completed, you can view the build results in the Releases tab.

4.3 Building and Packaging Applications in Azure DevOps

In Azure DevOps, you can create what are called "build pipelines" to automate the process of building your applications. You can also create "release pipelines" to automate the process of deploying your applications to different environments.

Creating a build pipeline is relatively simple. You just need to specify the source code repository that contains your application code, and then specify the steps that need to be executed in order to build the application. These steps can include things like compiling the code, running tests, and packaging the application.

Creating a release pipeline is a bit more complex, but still relatively straightforward. You need to specify the build pipeline that will be used to create the application artifacts, and then specify the steps that need to be executed in order to deploy the application to different environments. These steps can include things like provisioning resources in the target environment, deploying the application code, and running tests.

Both build pipelines and release pipelines can be configured to run automatically, or they can be manually triggered.

One of the great things about using Azure DevOps for your application development is that it makes it easy to set up a continuous delivery pipeline. This means that you can automatically deploy your application to different environments whenever a new change is made to the code base. This can save you a lot of time and effort, and it can help to ensure that your application is always up-to-date.

4.4 Running Automated Tests in Pipelines in Azure DevOps

As a developer, it is important to ensure that your code is working as intended before it is deployed to production. One way to do this is to use automated tests.

In Azure DevOps, you can set up a pipeline to run your automated tests as part of the build process. This way, you can be sure that your code is working as expected before it is deployed to production.

To set up a pipeline to run your automated tests, you will need to add a few steps to your existing pipeline. First, you will need to add a task to run your tests. There are many different ways to do this, but one option is to use the Visual Studio Test task.

Once you have added the task to run your tests, you will need to specify the path to your test assembly. You can do this by using the Assembly File Path setting.

Finally, you will need to specify the path to your test results file. This is important so that Azure DevOps can track your test results and provide you with feedback.

Once you have added these steps to your pipeline, you will be able to run your automated tests as part of the build process. This will help you to ensure that your code is working as expected before it is deployed to production.

4.5 Managing Pipeline Environments and Variables in Azure DevOps

When working with Azure DevOps, it's important to manage your pipeline environments and variables in order to keep your deployments consistent. There are a few different ways to do this, and the best approach will vary depending on your specific needs.

One way to manage your pipeline environments and variables is to use Azure DevOps Projects. With Azure DevOps Projects, you can easily create and manage environments for your pipelines. You can also use Azure DevOps Projects to manage your variables, and you can even use it to automate the creation and management of your pipeline environments.

Another way to manage your pipeline environments and variables is to use Azure DevOps Services. Azure DevOps Services provides a web-based interface for managing your pipelines and variables. You can also use Azure DevOps Services to automate the creation and management of your pipeline environments.

Finally, you can also use the Azure DevOps CLI to manage your pipeline environments and variables. The Azure DevOps CLI is a powerful tool that allows you to automate the creation and management of your pipeline environments.

No matter which method you choose to manage your pipeline environments and variables, the important thing is to make sure that you have a consistent and reliable process in place. By following these tips, you can ensure that your Azure DevOps deployments are always consistent and reliable.

Chapter 5: Azure Pipelines (Part 2: Advanced Topics)

5.1 Deploying Applications with Release Pipelines in Azure DevOps

As your application grows, you will need to deploy it with greater frequency. Azure DevOps provides release pipelines to help you automate this process.

Release pipelines are composed of two main elements:

1. The build pipeline, which packages your code into a deployable form

2. The release pipeline, which defines the steps necessary to deploy your application

Release pipelines are triggered by commits to your code repository. When a commit is made, the build pipeline is triggered and produces a deployable package. The release pipeline then takes this package and deploys it to your chosen environment.

Release pipelines can be configured to deploy to multiple environments, such as development, staging, and production. This allows you to test your application in each environment before making it available to users.

Release pipelines can also be configured to automatically roll back to a previous version if an error is detected in the current version. This ensures that your users always have a working version of your application.

Azure DevOps makes it easy to create and manage release pipelines. To learn more, see the Azure DevOps documentation.

5.2 Creating Environments and Managing Deployment Strategies in Azure DevOps

In Azure DevOps, you can create multiple environments for your applications, each with its own deployment strategy. For example, you could have a development environment where code changes are deployed automatically and a production environment where code changes are manually approved before being deployed.

You can also specify different deployment strategies for different types of code changes. For example, you could have a policy that automatically deploys code changes that are labeled as "hotfixes" but requires manual approval for code changes that are labeled as "features".

Creating multiple environments and specifying different deployment strategies helps you to control the risk of code changes and ensures that your applications are always running in a stable and predictable manner.

5.3 Automating Infrastructure Provisioning and Deployment in Azure DevOps

Infrastructure provisioning and deployment can be automated using Azure DevOps. This allows for a more consistent and repeatable process, as well as reducing the chances of human error.

In Azure DevOps, there are two main ways to automate infrastructure provisioning and deployment: using Azure Resource Manager (ARM) templates, or using Azure PowerShell.

ARM templates are JSON files that define the infrastructure and configuration for an Azure resource. Using ARM templates in Azure DevOps is a two-step process. First, the template must be added to the Azure DevOps repository. Second, an

Azure Pipeline must be created that uses the template to provision and deploy the resources.

Azure PowerShell is a scripting language that can be used to automate many tasks in Azure, including infrastructure provisioning and deployment. Azure PowerShell scripts can be added to an Azure DevOps repository and then run as part of an Azure Pipeline.

Both ARM templates and Azure PowerShell can be used to automate the provisioning and deployment of Azure resources. However, ARM templates are generally considered to be the more robust and recommended approach.

5.4 Implementing Approval Gates and Release Policies in Azure DevOps

When implementing approval gates and release policies in Azure DevOps, it is important to consider the following:

1. What is the purpose of the approval gate or release policy?

2. What are the conditions that must be met in order for the approval gate or release policy to be triggered?

3. Who will be responsible for approving or rejecting the request?

The purpose of an approval gate is to ensure that a specific condition or set of conditions is met before allowing a release to proceed. For example, an approval gate may be used to ensure that a code review has been completed and approved before allowing the code to be deployed to production.

The conditions that must be met in order for an approval gate to be triggered can be defined by the user. For example, the user may specify that the approval gate should be triggered when a code review has been completed and approved. Alternatively, the user may specify that the approval gate should be triggered when a specific user or group of users approves the request.

The person or persons responsible for approving or rejecting the request will depend on the specific approval gate or release policy. For example, if the approval gate is triggered when a code review has been completed, the code review team may be responsible for approving or rejecting the request. Alternatively, if the approval gate is triggered when a specific user or group of users approves the request, the user or group may be responsible for approving or rejecting the request.

5.5 Monitoring and Troubleshooting Pipelines in Azure DevOps

When it comes to monitoring and troubleshooting pipelines in Azure DevOps, there are a few key things to keep in mind. First and foremost, it is important to have a clear understanding of the pipeline itself and how it works. Secondly, it is important to have a clear understanding of the data that is being processed by the pipeline. Lastly, it is important to have a clear understanding of the tools and techniques that are available for monitoring and troubleshooting pipelines.

With that said, let's take a closer look at each of these three areas.

When it comes to understanding the pipeline itself, it is important to know the different stages that are involved in the pipeline. For example, in the case of a build pipeline, there are typically four stages: build, test, package, and deploy. Each stage has its own purpose and each stage can have its own set of tasks that need to be completed.

In terms of understanding the data that is being processed by the pipeline, it is important to know the format of the data and how it is being used by the pipeline. For example, if the data is in JSON format, then it is important to know how to parse

JSON data. Additionally, if the data is being used to trigger a build, then it is important to know how to trigger a build.

Finally, in terms of understanding the tools and techniques that are available for monitoring and troubleshooting pipelines, it is important to know the different types of logs that are available and how to use them. For example, Azure DevOps provides a variety of logs that can be used for monitoring and troubleshooting pipelines, including build logs, test logs, and package logs. Additionally, there are a number of third-party tools that can be used for monitoring and troubleshooting pipelines, such as New Relic and AppDynamics.

Chapter 6: Azure Test Plans

6.1 Overview of Azure Test Plans and Test Management in Azure DevOps

Azure Test Plans and Test Management is a powerful combination that can help developers ensure the quality of their applications. Test Plans provide a centralized location for managing all aspects of testing, including test cases, test suites, and test runs. Test Management in Azure DevOps allows developers to track and manage all aspects of their testing process, including test cases, test suites, test runs, and results. By using these two tools together, developers can more easily and effectively manage the quality of their applications.

6.2 Creating Test Plans and Test Suites in Azure DevOps

As a Quality Assurance Engineer, it is important to create test plans and test suites in Azure DevOps to ensure that the software development process is running smoothly. In this chapter, we will learn how to create a test plan and test suite in Azure DevOps.

Creating a test plan is simple. First, go to the Azure DevOps website and sign in. Then, click on the "Projects" tab and select the project you want to work on. Next, click on the "Test Plans" tab and select "New Test Plan".

Give your test plan a name and description, then click "Create".

Now that your test plan has been created, you can add test suites to it. To do this, click on the "Test Suites" tab and select "New Test Suite".

Give your test suite a name and description, then click "Create".

You can now add tests to your test suite. To do this, click on the "Tests" tab and select "New Test".

Give your test a name and description, then click "Create".

You can now run your tests and see the results. To do this, click on the "Run Tests" tab and select "Run".

You will see the results of your tests in the "Test Results" tab.

6.3 Test Case Management and Execution in Azure DevOps

As a member of the development team, I am responsible for ensuring that our products are thoroughly tested before they are released to our customers. To do this, I use Azure DevOps to manage our test cases and execute our testing plans.

Azure DevOps makes it easy to create and manage test cases, as well as to track and report on their results. I can easily see which test cases have been run, and which ones have failed, so that I can focus my attention on the areas that need the most attention.

Executing our testing plans in Azure DevOps is also straightforward. I can simply select the test cases that I want to run, and Azure DevOps will automatically execute them and provide me with the results. This makes it easy to keep our testing process organized and efficient.

Overall, Azure DevOps is a valuable tool for managing and executing our testing process. It helps me to ensure that our products are thoroughly tested before they are released to our customers, and makes it easy to track and report on the results of our testing.

6.4 Exploratory Testing and Session-based Testing in Azure DevOps

Exploratory testing is a type of testing that is conducted without pre-determined test cases or test scripts. It is a more flexible approach to testing, and allows testers to use their creativity and expertise to find bugs and issues that may not be found using traditional methods.

Session-based testing is a type of exploratory testing that is conducted in short, time-boxed sessions. This approach helps to structure the testing process and allows testers to focus on specific areas or goals for each session.

Both exploratory testing and session-based testing can be used in Azure DevOps to find bugs and issues in your applications. To get started, create a new test plan in Azure DevOps and select the type of testing you want to conduct. Then, create a new test case and select the type of test you want to run. For exploratory testing, you can simply select the "Exploratory" type. For session-based testing, you will need to select the "Session-based" type and specify the duration of the session.

Once you have created your test case, you can add it to a test suite and run it as part of your testing process. You can also use Azure DevOps to track the progress of your testing and to view results.

6.5 Integrating Automated Testing in Test Plans in Azure DevOps

As your application grows, the number of tests required to thoroughly test all the functionality can increase exponentially. To keep your test suite from becoming unmanageable, you can automate some of the tests. Doing so can also improve the reliability of your tests, since automated tests can be run more frequently and with more consistent results.

In Azure DevOps, you can automate your tests by adding them to a test plan. To do so, first create a new test plan or open an existing one. Then, in the left sidebar, select the Automated Tests tab.

Click the Add button to add a new automated test. You will be prompted to select the type of test you want to add. For this example, we will select a unit test.

Unit tests are code that test the functionality of your application at the individual class or method level. To add a unit test, you will need to provide a name and description for the test, as well as the path to the test assembly. You can also specify any additional settings for the test, such as the test category or priority.

Once you have added your unit test, it will appear in the list of tests for the plan. You can then run the test by selecting it and clicking the Run button. The results of the test will be displayed in the test results pane.

You can also add other types of automated tests to your plan, such as web performance tests or load tests. These tests can be used to simulate real-world conditions and test the scalability of your application.

To learn more about automating your tests in Azure DevOps, check out the documentation.

Chapter 7: Azure Artifacts

7.1 Introduction to Azure Artifacts and Package Management

Azure Artifacts is a cloud-based package management service that helps you share, discover, and reuse software packages across your development teams. Package management is a critical part of any software development process, and Azure Artifacts makes it easy to manage packages for your applications.

With Azure Artifacts, you can create and host your own package repositories, or use existing public repositories. You can also use Azure Artifacts to share packages across your development teams, and manage package dependencies for your applications.

Azure Artifacts is easy to use, and integrates with your existing development tools and processes. You can use Azure Artifacts with your favorite development tools, such as Visual Studio, Eclipse, and IntelliJ IDEA.

If you're new to package management, or just getting started with Azure Artifacts, this chapter will help you get started. We'll cover the basics of package management, and show you how to create and host your own package repositories. We'll also show you how to share packages across your development teams, and manage package dependencies for your applications.

7.2 Setting Up Package Feeds and NuGet Repositories in Azure DevOps

In order to set up a package feed and NuGet repository in Azure DevOps, you will need to first create a new Azure DevOps project. Once you have created the project, you will need to navigate to the "Artifacts" section and click on "Package Feeds". From here, you will need to click on the "New Feed" button and fill out the required information. Once you have created the feed, you will need to click on the "Connect to Feed" button and follow the instructions.

Once you have connected to the feed, you will need to navigate to the "Packages" section and click on the "New Package" button. From here, you will need to fill out the required information and upload the NuGet package. Once the package has been uploaded, you will need to click on the "Publish" button.

Once the package has been published, you will need to navigate to the "Repositories" section and click on the "New Repository" button. From here, you will need to fill out the required information and select the package feed that you created earlier. Once you have created the repository, you will need to click on the "Connect to Repository" button and follow the instructions.

Once you have connected to the repository, you will be able to view the NuGet packages that you have published. You can also view the package feed and NuGet repository in Azure DevOps by navigating to the "Artifacts" section and clicking on the "Package Feeds" and "Repositories" tabs.

7.3 Publishing and Managing Packages in Azure DevOps

Azure DevOps provides a rich set of tools for publishing and managing packages, making it easy to share code across teams and projects. In this section, we'll cover how to create and publish packages in Azure DevOps, and how to manage them using Azure Artifacts.

Creating a Package

To create a new package in Azure DevOps, navigate to the Packages page and select the New Package button. This will open the New Package dialog, where you can select the type of package you'd like to create. For this example, we'll choose the ASP.NET Core package type.

Once you've selected the package type, fill in the required fields and click the Create Package button. This will create a new package with the specified name and version.

Publishing a Package

Once you've created a package, you'll need to publish it so that it can be shared with others. To do this, navigate to the package's page and select the Publish Package button. This will open the Publish Package dialog, where you can specify the package's target feed.

Select the feed you want to publish the package to and click the Publish Package button. This will publish the package to the specified feed, making it available to others.

Managing Packages

Azure Artifacts provides a rich set of tools for managing packages. You can view information about published packages, such as their dependencies and versions. You can also manage packages using Azure Artifacts' powerful command-line interface.

To view information about a package, navigate to the package's page and select the View Package button. This will open the Package Details page, which provides a wealth of information about the package.

To manage a package using the Azure Artifacts CLI, install the Azure Artifacts CLI extension. Once you've installed the extension, you can use the az artifacts command to manage packages. For example, you can use the az artifacts package list command to list all of the packages in a feed.

Conclusion

In this section, we've covered how to create, publish, and manage packages using Azure DevOps. Azure DevOps makes it easy to share code across teams and projects, and Azure Artifacts provides a rich set of tools for managing packages.

7.4 Package Versioning and Dependency Management in Azure DevOps

Azure DevOps provides package versioning and dependency management capabilities that help you keep track of the versions of your software components and their dependencies. You can use these capabilities to manage the development and release process of your software applications.

Package versioning allows you to track the versions of your software components and their dependencies. You can use package versioning to manage the development and release process of your software applications.

Dependency management allows you to manage the dependencies of your software components. You can use dependency management to manage the development and release process of your software applications.

7.5 Integrating Artifacts with Build and Release Pipelines in Azure DevOps

Azure Artifacts is a service that helps developers manage software dependencies and share artifacts across their development teams. Azure DevOps provides a build and release pipeline that can be used to automatically build, test, and deploy software to Azure Artifacts.

In order to use Azure Artifacts with Azure DevOps, developers first need to create an Azure Artifacts account and configure it with their Azure DevOps organization. Once the account is configured, developers can create Azure Artifacts feeds and add artifacts to them.

Azure Artifacts feeds can be used to manage dependencies for both .NET and Java applications. For .NET applications, developers can use NuGet to add dependencies to their feeds. For Java applications, developers can use Maven to add dependencies to their feeds.

Once dependencies have been added to an Azure Artifacts feed, they can be used in Azure DevOps build and release pipelines. Build pipelines can be used to automatically build and test software. Release pipelines can be used to automatically deploy software to Azure Artifacts.

Azure Artifacts makes it easy for developers to manage software dependencies and share artifacts across their development teams. Azure DevOps provides a build and release pipeline that can be used to automatically build, test, and deploy software to Azure Artifacts.

Chapter 8: Azure DevOps Extensions and Integrations

8.1 Extending Azure DevOps with Marketplace Extensions

The Azure DevOps Marketplace is a great place to find extensions and integrations to help extend the functionality of your Azure DevOps account. In this chapter, we will take a look at some of the most popular Marketplace extensions and how they can be used to improve your Azure DevOps experience.

One of the most popular Marketplace extensions is the Azure DevOps Extension for Visual Studio Code. This extension allows you to connect to your Azure DevOps account and manage your repositories, work items, and builds directly from within Visual Studio Code. This is a great way to get started with Azure DevOps if you are already familiar with Visual Studio Code.

Another popular Marketplace extension is the Azure DevOps Extension for Microsoft Edge. This extension allows you to view your Azure DevOps account in Microsoft Edge, and also includes a number of useful features such as the ability to view work items and builds in the browser.

If you are looking for an extension that will help you to automate some of the tasks in Azure DevOps, then the Azure DevOps Extension for PowerShell is a great option. This extension allows you to run PowerShell scripts directly from within Azure DevOps, and can be used to automate a variety of tasks such as creating work items, triggering builds, and more.

Finally, if you are looking for an extension that will help you to integrate Azure DevOps with other applications, then the Azure DevOps Extension for Zapier is a great option. This extension allows you to connect Azure DevOps with a variety of other applications, such as Slack, Jira, and more.

In conclusion, the Azure DevOps Marketplace is a great place to find extensions and integrations to help extend the functionality of your Azure DevOps account. There are a variety of extensions available, each of which can be used to improve your Azure DevOps experience in a different way.

8.2 Exploring Commonly Used Extensions in Azure DevOps

As an Azure DevOps engineer, it is important to be familiar with the various extensions and integrations that are available. In this chapter, we will explore some of the most commonly used extensions.

One of the most popular extensions is the Azure DevOps Extension for Visual Studio Code. This extension allows you to connect to your Azure DevOps account and manage your repositories, work items, and builds.

Another popular extension is the Azure DevOps Extension for Azure CLI. This extension allows you to interact with Azure DevOps using the Azure CLI.

There are also a number of extensions that allow you to integrate Azure DevOps with other tools and services. For example, there is an extension for Jenkins that allows you to trigger Jenkins builds from Azure DevOps. There is also an extension for Slack that allows you to receive notifications about Azure DevOps events in Slack.

Finally, there are a number of extensions that add additional functionality to Azure DevOps. For example, there is an extension that allows you to view GitHub repositories within Azure DevOps. There is also an extension that allows you to add custom widgets to the Azure DevOps dashboards.

No matter what your needs are, there is likely an extension or integration that can help you. Be sure to explore the options that are available to you and take advantage of the power of Azure DevOps extensions and integrations.

8.3 Creating Custom Extensions for Azure DevOps

If you're looking to extend the functionality of Azure DevOps, you can do so by creating custom extensions. There are a few different ways to go about this, but the end result is the same: you'll have a custom-built extension that integrates with Azure DevOps and provides the functionality you need.

The first thing you'll need to do is decide what kind of extension you want to create. There are four different types of extensions:

Task Extensions: These extensions allow you to add new build or release tasks to Azure DevOps.

Service Endpoint Extensions: These extensions allow you to add new service endpoints to Azure DevOps.

Dashboard Extensions: These extensions allow you to add new widgets to Azure DevOps dashboards.

Build & Release Agent Extensions: These extensions allow you to add new build and release agents to Azure DevOps.

Once you've decided on the type of extension you want to create, you'll need to choose a programming language. Azure DevOps extensions can be written in either JavaScript or TypeScript.

Once you've chosen a programming language, you'll need to set up your development environment. The Azure DevOps Extension SDK makes it easy to set up a development environment, regardless of which programming language you're using.

Once you have your development environment set up, you'll need to write the code for your extension. The Azure DevOps Extension SDK provides a set of APIs that you can use to interact with Azure DevOps.

Once you've written the code for your extension, you'll need to package it up and publish it to the Azure DevOps Marketplace. The Azure DevOps

Marketplace is the central repository for Azure DevOps extensions.

Once your extension is published to the Azure DevOps Marketplace, anyone can install and use it. If you want to restrict who can install and use your extension, you can do so by setting a price for your extension.

Creating a custom extension for Azure DevOps is a great way to extend the functionality of Azure DevOps. The Azure DevOps Extension SDK makes it easy to get started, and the Azure DevOps Marketplace provides a central repository for extensions.

8.4 Integrating Azure DevOps with Third-Party Tools and Services

Azure DevOps is a powerful platform for managing development workflows. One of the benefits of using Azure DevOps is the ability to integrate with a variety of third-party tools and services. This allows organizations to use the best tool for the job, while still being able to take advantage of the powerful Azure DevOps platform.

In this chapter, we will take a look at how to integrate Azure DevOps with third-party tools and services. We will start by looking at how to integrate with GitHub, one of the most popular code hosting platforms. Then, we will look at how to integrate with Slack, a popular team chat application. Finally, we will look at how to integrate with Jira, a popular issue tracking tool.

GitHub Integration

Azure DevOps can be integrated with GitHub in a few different ways. The first way is through the GitHub Marketplace. The GitHub Marketplace is a place where developers can find and install third-party applications and services that integrate with GitHub. There are a number of different Azure DevOps extensions available on the GitHub Marketplace, which makes it easy to get started with Azure DevOps and GitHub integration.

The second way to integrate Azure DevOps with GitHub is through the GitHub API. The GitHub API allows developers to access Azure DevOps data and functionality from within their own applications. This is a powerful way to build custom integrations between Azure DevOps and GitHub.

Slack Integration

Slack is a popular team chat application that can be integrated with Azure DevOps. There are a few different ways to integrate Slack with Azure DevOps. The first way is through the Slack Marketplace. The Slack Marketplace is a place where developers can find and install third-party applications and services that integrate with Slack. There are a number of different Azure DevOps extensions available on the Slack Marketplace, which makes it easy to get started with Azure DevOps and Slack integration.

The second way to integrate Azure DevOps with Slack is through the Slack API. The Slack API allows developers to access Azure DevOps data and functionality from within their own applications. This is a powerful way to build custom integrations between Azure DevOps and Slack.

Jira Integration

Jira is a popular issue tracking tool that can be integrated with Azure DevOps. There are a few different ways to integrate Jira with Azure DevOps. The first way is through the Jira Marketplace. The Jira Marketplace is a place where developers can find and install third-party applications and services that integrate with Jira. There are a number of different Azure DevOps extensions available on the Jira Marketplace, which makes it easy to get started with Azure DevOps and Jira integration.

The second way to integrate Azure DevOps with Jira is through the Jira API. The Jira API allows developers to access Azure DevOps data and functionality from within their own applications. This is a powerful way to build custom integrations between Azure DevOps and Jira.

Chapter 9: Infrastructure as Code with Azure DevOps

9.1 Introduction to Infrastructure as Code (IaC) Concepts in Azure DevOps

Infrastructure as code (IaC) is the process of managing and provisioning computer data centers through machine-readable definition files, rather than physical hardware configuration.

IaC is an approach to infrastructure management that treats infrastructure as a software entity that can be versioned, audited, and managed using the same tools and processes as application code.

Azure DevOps is a set of services that help developers ship high-quality products faster by enabling them to collaborate and automate the build, test, and deploy process.

Azure DevOps provides a set of built-in tasks that allow you to easily provision and configure Azure resources, such as web apps, databases, and VMs.

In this chapter, you will learn about the following IaC concepts in Azure DevOps:

- YAML pipelines

- Azure Resource Manager (ARM) templates
- Azure CLI
- Azure PowerShell

YAML pipelines are a way to define your build, test, and deploy process in a single file that can be stored in your source control repository.

Azure Resource Manager (ARM) templates are a declarative way to provision and configure Azure resources.

Azure CLI is a command-line interface that you can use to manage Azure resources.

Azure PowerShell is a PowerShell module that you can use to manage Azure resources.

9.2 Managing Infrastructure Deployments with Azure Resource Manager (ARM) Templates in Azure DevOps

Azure Resource Manager (ARM) templates are a great way to manage infrastructure deployments in Azure DevOps. By using ARM templates, you can define your infrastructure as code and then manage and deploy it using Azure DevOps. This makes it easy to track changes to your infrastructure and to ensure that your infrastructure is always up-to-date.

To use ARM templates in Azure DevOps, you first need to create a new Azure DevOps project. Then, you need to add a new ARM template to your project. To do this, click on the "Add" button in the Azure DevOps project, and then select "Add ARM Template."

Once you have added the ARM template to your project, you can edit it to define your infrastructure. The ARM template syntax is similar to JSON, so it is easy to learn and to use. Once you have defined your infrastructure, you can then deploy it using Azure DevOps.

To deploy your infrastructure, you first need to create a new Azure DevOps release. To do this, click on the "Releases" tab in Azure DevOps, and then click on the "New Release" button.

In the "New Release" dialog, you will need to specify a name for your release and a description. You will also need to select the ARM template that you want to deploy. Once you have done this, click on the "Create" button.

Once your release has been created, you can then deploy it. To do this, click on the "Deploy" button in the Azure DevOps release.

In the "Deploy" dialog, you will need to specify the environment in which you want to deploy your infrastructure. You will also need to specify the Azure subscription that you want to use. Once you have done this, click on the "Deploy" button.

Once the deployment has started, you can monitor its progress in the Azure DevOps release. You can also view the output of the deployment in the "Output" tab.

Once the deployment has completed, you can view the results in the "Results" tab.

ARM templates are a great way to manage infrastructure deployments in Azure DevOps. By using ARM templates, you can define your infrastructure as code and then manage and deploy it using Azure DevOps. This makes it easy to track changes to your infrastructure and to ensure that your infrastructure is always up-to-date.

9.3 Configuring Continuous Deployment for Infrastructure in Azure DevOps

Continuous deployment for infrastructure in Azure DevOps is a great way to ensure that your infrastructure is always up-to-date and compliant with your organization's standards. By configuring continuous deployment, you can automatically trigger a release when changes are made to your infrastructure code. This allows you to quickly and easily deploy changes to your infrastructure, without having to manually trigger a release.

To configure continuous deployment for infrastructure in Azure DevOps, you first need to create a release pipeline. Release pipelines are used to automate the process of releasing software changes to a staging or production environment. To create a release pipeline, navigate to the Releases tab in Azure DevOps and click "New pipeline".

Next, you will need to select a template for your release pipeline. For this example, we will use the "Empty job" template.

Once you have selected a template, you will need to configure your release pipeline. In the "Stage 1" section, click "Add an artifact". Artifacts are the files that will be deployed as part of your release. In this case, we will add the Azure Resource Manager template for our infrastructure as our artifact.

Next, you will need to configure your trigger. The trigger determines when a release will be automatically triggered. In this case, we will configure our trigger to fire when changes are made to our Azure Resource Manager template.

Finally, you will need to configure your deployment. The deployment is responsible for actually deploying the changes to your infrastructure. In this case, we will use the Azure Resource Manager Deployment task to deploy our changes.

Once you have configured your release pipeline, you can save it and queue a new release. Azure DevOps will automatically trigger a release when changes are made to your Azure Resource Manager template. This allows you to quickly and easily deploy changes to your infrastructure, without having to manually trigger a release.

9.4 Infrastructure Testing and Validation in Azure DevOps

As organizations move towards a DevOps model, the need to test and validate infrastructure changes becomes more important. Azure DevOps provides a set of tools to help with this process.

Infrastructure as code (IaC) is a way of managing infrastructure in a declarative, versionable, and repeatable manner. IaC tools allow operators to define infrastructure in a template or configuration file, which can then be used to provision and manage that infrastructure.

Azure DevOps provides a set of built-in tasks for infrastructure testing and validation as part of its release pipelines. These tasks can be used to run tests against infrastructure-as-code templates, to validate changes before they are deployed, and to generate reports on the results of the tests.

The infrastructure testing and validation tasks in Azure DevOps can be used to test a variety of infrastructure-as-code templates, including those for Azure Resource Manager (ARM), Terraform, and AWS CloudFormation.

The following are some of the tests that can be performed using these tasks:

- ARM template validation: Checks the syntax of an ARM template and verifies that all required parameters are provided.

- Terraform plan: Runs a Terraform plan and reports on any changes that would be made to the infrastructure.

- AWS CloudFormation template validation: Checks the syntax of an AWS CloudFormation template.

- AWS CloudFormation stack validation: Validates an AWS CloudFormation stack by checking that all required resources have been created and that all outputs are as expected.

- Azure Resource Group deployment: Deploys an Azure Resource Group and reports on any changes that were made.

These tasks can be run manually as part of a release pipeline or they can be configured to run automatically as part of an Azure DevOps Service hook.

Configuring these tasks to run automatically can help to ensure that infrastructure changes are properly tested and validated before they are deployed to production.

9.5 Infrastructure Monitoring and Compliance with Azure DevOps

The Azure DevOps platform provides a powerful set of tools for infrastructure monitoring and compliance. With Azure DevOps, you can monitor your infrastructure for changes and compliance issues, and take corrective action quickly and easily.

Azure DevOps provides a central location for monitoring your infrastructure. You can see all changes to your infrastructure in one place, and quickly identify and fix compliance issues. Azure DevOps also provides a rich set of tools for configuring and managing your infrastructure.

Azure DevOps makes it easy to monitor your infrastructure for changes. You can see all changes to your infrastructure in one place, and quickly identify and fix compliance issues. Azure DevOps also makes it easy to take corrective action quickly and easily.

Azure DevOps is a powerful platform for infrastructure monitoring and compliance. With Azure DevOps, you can monitor your infrastructure for changes and compliance issues, and take corrective action quickly and easily.

Chapter 10: DevOps Security and Compliance in Azure DevOps

10.1 Security Considerations in DevOps Processes in Azure DevOps

As organizations move to adopt DevOps processes in Azure DevOps, it is important to consider the security implications of these changes. In particular, Azure DevOps provides a number of features that can help to secure DevOps processes.

First, Azure DevOps provides a centralized place for managing security and compliance policies. This can help to ensure that all policies are consistently applied across the organization.

Second, Azure DevOps provides a number of built-in security controls, such as role-based access control and auditing. These controls can help to prevent unauthorized access to resources and to track changes made to resources.

Third, Azure DevOps can be integrated with other security tools, such as Azure Security Center. This integration can help to provide a comprehensive view of the security posture of an organization's Azure resources.

Finally, Azure DevOps provides a number of resources that can help organizations to understand and implement DevOps security best practices. These resources can help to ensure that DevOps processes are securely implemented in Azure DevOps.

10.2 Implementing Secure Development Practices in Azure DevOps

As organizations move to Azure DevOps, they need to implement secure development practices to ensure the security and compliance of their applications. Azure DevOps provides a set of built-in security controls that can be used to secure development environments and prevent data leaks.

Organizations can use Azure DevOps to control access to their development resources and restrict access to sensitive data. They can also use Azure DevOps to monitor activity and track changes to their code base. Azure DevOps can also be used to scan code for vulnerabilities and compliance issues.

Organizations should consider the security implications of every change to their code base

and make sure that they understand the risks
involved. They should also implement security
controls at every stage of the development
process. By doing so, they can ensure that their
applications are secure and compliant with
industry regulations.

10.3 Integrating Security Scanning and Vulnerability Management in Azure DevOps

As organizations move to Azure DevOps, it is
important to consider how to integrate security
scanning and vulnerability management into the
process. There are a number of ways to do this, but
one approach is to use Azure DevOps Security
Center.

Security Center can be used to scan for
vulnerabilities in your code and then track and
manage them over time. This can be done through
the use of security policies, which can be used to
automatically scan for vulnerabilities and then
track and remediate them.

To get started, you first need to create a security
policy in Security Center. This policy will define
what types of vulnerabilities you want to scan for
and how often you want the scan to run. Once the

policy is created, you can then add it to your Azure DevOps pipeline.

When the policy is added to the pipeline, it will automatically scan your code for vulnerabilities. If any are found, they will be reported in the security policy. You can then view the details of the vulnerabilities and decide how to remediate them.

Azure DevOps Security Center is a powerful tool that can help you integrate security scanning and vulnerability management into your Azure DevOps pipeline. By using security policies, you can automatically scan for vulnerabilities and then track and remediate them. This can help you keep your code secure and compliant with security standards.

10.4 Compliance and Audit Trail in Azure DevOps

As your organization starts to use Azure DevOps, you'll want to ensure that all users and processes are compliant with your company's policies and procedures. To help with this, Azure DevOps offers a compliance and audit trail feature. This feature provides a complete record of all activity within your Azure DevOps account, including who did what and when. This information can be used to help identify potential compliance issues and to investigate any suspicious activity. The compliance and audit trail feature is available to all users with an Azure DevOps account. To access the compliance and audit trail, simply go to the "Security" section of the Azure DevOps portal. From here, you can view a complete history of all activity within your account. You can also use the compliance and audit trail to generate reports on specific users, groups, or processes. This information can be used to help improve your company's overall compliance posture.

10.5 DevSecOps: Incorporating Security Throughout the DevOps Lifecycle in Azure DevOps

As organizations move to DevOps, they must also consider how to best integrate security into their new processes and workflows. DevSecOps is a term that refers to the incorporation of security throughout the DevOps lifecycle. By integrating security into all phases of the DevOps process, organizations can more effectively secure their applications and infrastructure.

In Azure DevOps, there are a number of features and services that can help organizations with their DevSecOps efforts. For example, Azure DevOps provides built-in support for security scanning and compliance reporting. Additionally, Azure DevOps offers a number of integrations with popular security tools, such as Azure Security Center and Azure Sentinel.

Organizations can use Azure DevOps to help them automate their security processes and workflows. By doing so, they can more effectively secure their applications and infrastructure, while also reducing the overhead associated with manual security tasks.

Chapter 11: Azure DevOps for Multi-team and Enterprise Environments

11.1 Scaling Azure DevOps for Large Projects and Multiple Teams

As organizations grow, they often need to scale their Azure DevOps projects and teams to meet their increasing needs. There are a number of ways to do this, and the most effective approach depends on the specific needs of the organization.

One common way to scale Azure DevOps for large projects and multiple teams is to use Azure DevOps Projects. This approach allows organizations to create multiple projects within a single Azure DevOps organization, each with its own set of teams and resources. This can be an effective way to manage large projects with multiple teams, as it allows each team to work on its own project with its own set of resources.

Another common way to scale Azure DevOps is to use Azure DevOps Groups. This approach allows organizations to create groups of users who have access to specific Azure DevOps resources. This can be an effective way to manage access to Azure

DevOps resources for large projects and multiple teams.

The most effective way to scale Azure DevOps for large projects and multiple teams depends on the specific needs of the organization. However, using Azure DevOps Projects and Azure DevOps Groups can be an effective way to manage large projects with multiple teams.

11.2 Managing Permissions and Access Control in Azure DevOps

Azure DevOps provides a set of tools and services that help software development teams manage the software development process. One of the key areas that Azure DevOps helps with is managing permissions and access control.

Permissions and access control in Azure DevOps help teams to control who has access to what resources and information. This is important in ensuring that only authorized users can access sensitive data and that teams can work together effectively.

There are a number of ways to manage permissions and access control in Azure DevOps.

Teams can control access at the project level, the repository level, and the branch level.

At the project level, teams can control who has access to the project and what they can do with the project. For example, teams can give certain users access to view project information, while others may have access to edit project information.

At the repository level, teams can control who has access to the code and what they can do with the code. For example, teams can give certain users access to view the code, while others may have access to edit the code.

At the branch level, teams can control who has access to the code in a particular branch. For example, teams can give certain users access to view the code in a particular branch, while others may have access to edit the code in that branch.

Permissions and access control in Azure DevOps help teams to work together effectively and to ensure that only authorized users can access sensitive data.

11.3 Configuring Branch Policies and Code Reviews for Collaboration in Azure DevOps

Branch policies and code reviews are two important features in Azure DevOps that can help teams to collaborate more effectively. By configuring branch policies, teams can define rules for how their code should be structured and formatted. This can help to ensure that all code is consistent and easy to read. Code reviews can also be used to check for errors and potential problems. By requiring all code changes to be reviewed by another team member, teams can avoid mistakes and ensure that everyone is on the same page.

11.4 Setting Up Governance and Compliance Standards in Azure DevOps

In order to set up governance and compliance standards in Azure DevOps, it is necessary to first understand what these terms mean. Governance refers to the process and framework by which an organization makes decisions. Compliance standards are the guidelines that an organization must follow in order to meet its legal and regulatory obligations.

There are a number of ways to set up governance and compliance standards in Azure DevOps. One way is to use Azure Policy. Azure Policy is a service that allows you to create and manage policies that enforce compliance standards on your Azure resources. Another way to set up governance and compliance standards in Azure DevOps is to use Azure Resource Manager templates. Resource Manager templates are JSON files that define the resources that should be deployed to Azure. You can use Resource Manager templates to enforce compliance standards by specifying which resources should be deployed and how they should be configured.

Once you have decided how you want to set up governance and compliance standards in Azure DevOps, you will need to create a policy or template that defines the standards that you want to enforce. Once you have created your policy or template, you will need to assign it to the appropriate team or organization. Once your policy or template has been assigned, it will be enforced on all resources that are deployed to Azure.

11.5 Implementing DevOps Best Practices in Enterprise Environments in Azure DevOps

As enterprises move to adopt DevOps practices, Azure DevOps provides a comprehensive set of tools and services to support these efforts. In this chapter, we will discuss how to implement DevOps best practices in enterprise environments using Azure DevOps.

We will start by looking at how to setup Azure DevOps to support multiple teams and projects. We will then discuss how to use Azure DevOps to manage and deploy enterprise applications. Finally, we will look at how to use Azure DevOps to monitor and troubleshoot enterprise applications.

Multi-team and project support in Azure DevOps

Azure DevOps provides comprehensive support for multi-team and multi-project environments. Organizations can use Azure DevOps to setup separate projects for each team, and then use Azure DevOps to manage the dependencies between these projects.

Azure DevOps also provides powerful reporting and analytics capabilities to help organizations track the progress of their multi-team and multi-project efforts.

Enterprise application management and deployment

Azure DevOps provides a complete set of tools and services for managing and deploying enterprise applications. Organizations can use Azure DevOps to manage application lifecycles, deploy applications to multiple environments, and monitor the health of enterprise applications.

Azure DevOps also provides extensive support for Continuous Delivery and Continuous Deployment pipelines. Organizations can use Azure DevOps to automate the build, testing, and deployment of their enterprise applications.

Monitoring and troubleshooting enterprise applications

Azure DevOps provides a complete set of tools and services for monitoring and troubleshooting enterprise applications. Organizations can use Azure DevOps to monitor the performance of their applications, and to identify and diagnose problems.

Azure DevOps also provides extensive support for logging and tracing. Organizations can use Azure DevOps to collect and analyze application logs, and to troubleshoot application problems.

Chapter 12: Continuous Improvement and Future Trends in Azure DevOps

12.1 Embracing a Culture of Continuous Improvement in Azure DevOps

The Azure DevOps platform is built on the principle of continuous improvement. This means that the platform is constantly evolving to meet the ever-changing needs of developers and organizations. The Azure DevOps team is constantly working to improve the platform and make it more user-friendly and efficient. In addition, the team is always looking for ways to improve the platform's functionality and add new features that will make it even more valuable to developers and organizations.

12.2 Monitoring and Analyzing DevOps Metrics and Performance in Azure DevOps

As the world of software development changes and evolves, so too must the way in which we monitor and analyze the performance of our systems. In

Azure DevOps, we have a wealth of tools and capabilities at our disposal to help us do just that.

In this chapter, we will take a look at some of the ways in which we can monitor and analyze the performance of our DevOps processes and systems in Azure DevOps. We will also touch on some of the future trends that we can expect to see in this area.

So, let's get started!

As our systems grow and become more complex, it is important that we have ways to monitor their performance so that we can identify and fix any issues that may arise.

Azure DevOps provides us with a number of built-in tools and services that we can use for this purpose. For example, we can use the Azure Monitor service to collect and analyze performance data from our Azure resources.

We can also use the Azure Log Analytics service to collect and analyze log data from our systems. This can be extremely useful for troubleshooting purposes.

In addition to these built-in services, there are a number of third-party tools and services that we can use to supplement our monitoring and analysis efforts.

One such tool is New Relic, which provides us with comprehensive performance monitoring capabilities.

Another popular tool is AppDynamics, which offers similar functionality to New Relic.

There are many other tools and services available, so be sure to explore what is out there and find the ones that best fit your needs.

As we mentioned earlier, monitoring and analyzing the performance of our systems is only half of the equation. The other half is taking action to improve the performance of our systems.

There are a number of ways in which we can do this in Azure DevOps. For example, we can use the Azure Pipelines service to automate the deployment of our code changes.

We can also use the Azure Boards service to help us track and manage our work items.

And, of course, we can always use the good old-fashioned manual process of code review and testing to find and fix performance issues.

No matter what approach we take, the important thing is that we continuously strive to improve the performance of our systems.

As we have seen, Azure DevOps provides us with a wealth of tools and capabilities for monitoring and analyzing the performance of our systems. In addition, it also provides us with the ability to take action to improve the performance of our systems.

So, what does the future hold for Azure DevOps?

As the world of software development continues to change and evolve, so too will Azure DevOps. We can expect to see new features and capabilities added to Azure DevOps on a regular basis.

We can also expect to see more and more integration between Azure DevOps and other Microsoft products and services.

So, what does that mean for us?

Simply put, it means that Azure DevOps is here to stay and that it is only going to get better with time.

So, if you are not already using Azure DevOps, now is the time to get onboard!

12.3 Identifying and Addressing Bottlenecks in the Azure DevOps Workflow

The Azure DevOps workflow is designed to be highly efficient, but there are always potential bottlenecks that can slow things down. In this chapter, we'll take a look at some of the most common bottlenecks and how to address them.

One of the most common bottlenecks is the lack of a clear workflow. When developers are working on a project, they need to know what the next steps are and what needs to be done in order to move the project forward. Without a clear workflow, developers can get bogged down and the project can stall.

Another common bottleneck is inadequate testing. Before code is deployed to production, it needs to be thoroughly tested. If there are bugs in the code, they can cause major problems down the line. In order to avoid this, it's important to have a robust testing process in place.

Finally, another potential bottleneck is poor communication. When developers are working on a project, they need to be able to communicate with each other in order to make sure that everyone is on the same page. If communication breaks down, it can lead to misunderstandings and delays.

Fortunately, there are ways to address these bottlenecks. By having a clear workflow, adequate testing, and good communication, you can keep your Azure DevOps projects moving forward smoothly.

12.4 DevOps Trends and Innovations

DevOps is an ever-evolving field with new trends and innovations popping up all the time. It can be hard to keep up with all the latest developments, but it's important to stay abreast of the latest trends in order to stay ahead of the curve.

Some of the latest DevOps trends and innovations include:

1. Containers and microservices

Containers and microservices are becoming increasingly popular in the world of DevOps. They allow for greater flexibility and scalability, and can make it easier to manage complex applications.

2. ChatOps

ChatOps is a relatively new trend that is gaining popularity. It involves using chatbots to help manage and automate tasks related to DevOps. This can help to improve communication and collaboration within a DevOps team.

3. Serverless architecture

Serverless architecture is another trend that is on the rise. This type of architecture can help to improve scalability and reduce costs.

4. Artificial intelligence and machine learning

Artificial intelligence (AI) and machine learning are two technologies that are starting to be used more and more in DevOps. They can help to automate tasks and improve decision-making.

5. Security

Security is always a top concern in DevOps. With the increasing use of containers and microservices, it's important to ensure that these technologies are properly secured.

These are just a few of the latest trends and innovations in DevOps. As the field continues to evolve, there will no doubt be many more exciting developments to come.

12.5 Enhancing Collaboration and Integration with Azure DevOps

Azure DevOps is a cloud-based service that provides an end-to-end DevOps solution for developing and deploying applications. It includes a set of developer tools, services, and build and release pipelines. Azure DevOps enables developers to collaborate and integrate their work with other teams. It also helps to automate the build and release process.

Azure DevOps has a lot of features that help to improve collaboration and integration. For example, Azure DevOps has a built-in Wiki that enables developers to share information and collaborate on documentation. Azure DevOps also has a built-in code editor that enables developers to edit code and collaborate on code changes. Azure DevOps also has a built-in issue tracker that enables developers to track and manage issues.

Azure DevOps also has a lot of features that help to automate the build and release process. For example, Azure DevOps can automatically build and deploy applications. Azure DevOps can also automatically run tests and generate reports. Azure DevOps can also automatically create and manage branches.

Azure DevOps is a powerful tool that can help to improve collaboration and integration. It has a lot of features that can help to automate the build and release process. It is a cloud-based service that provides an end-to-end DevOps solution.